| Writer | Karen L. Hill | contact@karenlHill.com |
| Illustrator | CJ Love | c.love2design@gmail.com |

I dedicate this book

to future generations

in a changing culture.

God affirms –

there are only two genders:

Male

and

Female

I am Male.

I am Female

*"But from the beginning of creation,
God made them male and female."
Mark 10:6 NIV*

2

I am "him."

I am "her."

"But 'God made them male and female' from the beginning of creation."   Mark 10:6

I am "he."

I am "she."

There are no other genders.

"Male and female he created them, and he blessed
them and named them Man when they were created."
Gen 5:2 ESV

God created us.

"So God created man in his own image,
in the image of God he created him;
male and female he created them."
Gen 1:27 ESV

God created both

male and female

to enjoy

and complement

one another.

God's design is that

a male and female

marry, raise a

family and govern

the earth together.

When I decide to get married, I will marry a female.

When I decide to marry, I will marry a male.

We will start a family.

*"That is why a man leaves his father and mother
and is united with his wife,
And they become one."*
Genesis 2:24 (GNT)

Science affirms –

there are only two genders:

Male

and

Female

I am male. The male gender is expressed
by the XY alphabets.

I am female. The female gender is
expressed by the XX alphabets.

This reality
is fixed at
conception.
It will not
change.

The body affirms –

there are only two genders:

Male

and

Female

I am male and my private parts are different from a female.

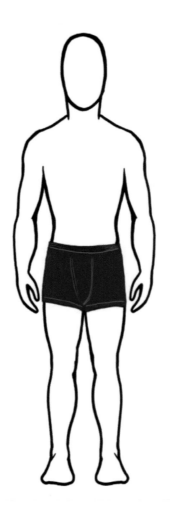

I am female and my private parts are different from a male.

I am male. My bones are generally longer and thicker in the arms, legs and fingers. I am usually stronger and larger than a female. I am unable to birth a baby.

I am female. My bones development is female. I'm softer than a male. My body is designed to accommodate the growth and delivery of a baby.

We cannot depend on
our emotions to
affirm -

that there are only two genders:

Male

and

Female

We cannot
depend on
our emotions
to confirm
who we are.

We cannot
live our lives
based on how
we feel.

Some days we are happy and confident.

Some days we are sad and lonely.

No matter

how we feel,

our gender

will not

change.

I am male and my gender
will not change based on
my feelings or the voices
I hear in my head.

I am female and my gender will not change based on the images I see on TV, in the movies, in my school, among my peers, community, church or the law of the land.

Our genders will not change based on
the events that may happen to us
as children.

No matter what,

I am male. I don't want to be a female.

No matter what,

I am female. I don't want to be a male.

The truth is –

*I am beautifully
and wonderfully made.*

I know that,
without a doubt.

THE END